D1146909

The Fabian Society is Britain's oldest political think tank. Since 1884 the Society has played a central role in developing political ideas and public policy on the left.

Through a wide range of publications and events the Society influences political and public thinking, but also provides a space for broad and open-minded debate, drawing on an unrivalled external network and its own expert research and analysis.

The Society is alone among think tanks in being a democratically-constituted membership organisation, with almost 7,000 members. During its history the membership has included many of the key thinkers on the British left and every Labour Prime Minister. Today it counts over 200 parliamentarians in its number. Member-led activity includes 70 local Fabian societies, the Scottish and Welsh Fabians, the Fabian Women's Network and the Young Fabians, which is itself the leading organisation on the left for young people to debate and influence political ideas.

The Society was one of the original founders of the Labour Party and is constitutionally affiliated to the party. It is however editorially, organisationally and financially independent and works with a wide range of partners of all political persuasions and none.

Fabian Society
61 Petty France
London SW1H 9EU
www.fabians.org.uk

Fabian Ideas 642

First published 2016
ISBN 978-0-7163-0642-9

Editorial Director: Ed Wallis
Research and Editorial Assistant: Tobias Phibbs

*This pamphlet, like all publications of the Fabian Society,
represents not the collective views of the Society but only the
views of the author. The responsibility of the Society is limited
to approving its publications as worthy of consideration within
the Labour movement. This publication may not be reproduced
without express permission of the Fabian Society.*

British Library Cataloguing in Publication data. A catalogue
record for this book is available from the British Library.

Printed and bound by DG3, London, UK

To find out more about the Fabian Society, the Young
Fabians, the Fabian Women's Network and our local
societies, please visit our website at www.fabians.org.uk.

Productive Purpose

Investment, competitiveness and the new economics

by Bryan Gould

About the author

Bryan Gould was a New Zealand Rhodes Scholar who has been variously a British diplomat, an Oxford law don, a television journalist, and Labour politician. He was elected as MP for Southampton Test in 1974 and for Dagenham in 1983. He joined the shadow cabinet in 1986, directed Labour's election campaign in 1987, and contested the Labour party leadership in 1992. In 1994, he returned to New Zealand as vice-chancellor of Waikato University.

Bryan Gould has co-authored a number of books, including *A Charter for the Disabled* (1981) and *Monetarism or Prosperity?* (1981). His other books include *Socialism and Freedom* (1985), *A Future for Socialism* (1989) and the autobiographical *Goodbye to All That* (1995). *The Democracy Sham: How Globalisation Devalues Your Vote* was published in September 2006, *Rescuing the New Zealand Economy* in 2007 and *Myths, Politicians and Money* in 2013.

CONTENTS

Acknowledgments

The author would like to thank John Mills for the collaboration they have enjoyed over 35 years (and some of whose fruits are to be seen in the later parts of this pamphlet) and for his support for the current project.

He would also like to thank George Tait Edwards, who has done so much to draw attention to the important work of Osamu Shimomura, Stewart Lansley and John Wrathmell for their helpful comments on the draft and the Fabian Society – and especially Ed Wallis – for their help and for their commitment to their longstanding mission to bring new thinking on the left to a wider readership.

The Fabian Society are grateful for the kind support of John Mills which made this publication possible.

The election of Jeremy Corbyn to the Labour leadership owed much to his argument that austerity is the wrong response to recession and that a successful economic policy should address the goals of improving our productive capacity and a fair distribution of the fruits of economic success.

The mere fact that these assertions have been made has changed the shape of the debate about both politics and economic policy. It has encouraged the growing emergence of a new mainstream consensus that at last offers a real alternative to neo-classical and 'free market' orthodoxy.

For those who welcome and support that development, however, there remain important questions to be answered about how 'Corbynomics' might work in practice. If we are to secure an economic future that relies on more than asset inflation and an unsustainable consumer boom, we first need a new approach to monetary policy so that the power of government can be used to stimulate much-needed investment in greater productive capacity and full employment. Second, any strategy for sustainable growth and increased investment will be frustrated unless the main inhibition to any policy for growth – the damaging and long-term loss of international competitiveness suffered by British industry – is overcome.

This pamphlet addresses both of these central issues and argues that they are interlinked. Increased productive investment and improved competitiveness are the twin pillars of a credible and coherent strategy that would revolutionise our economic prospects.

To put this into practice, the pamphlet makes the following recommendations:

Design a monetary policy for growth

- Money-creating power should be restored to the government, with the banks acting as the government's agents.
- Credit creation should be targeted at increasing investment in productive industry, with the goal of increasing productivity, accelerating the rate of economic growth and providing full employment.
- This policy of investment credit creation would benefit the economy *directly,* because of the increased money made available for investment in productive capacity; and *indirectly*, because the productive economy would be spared high interest rates and an overvalued currency.

Focus on productive investment

- The principal focus of a strategy that selectively applied credit creation to productive purposes would be the provision of cost-free or at least low-cost credit to productive industry.
- The most effective way of doing this would be to utilise the existing range of banking services but to ensure that they functioned and re-focused under the direction of the central bank and for purposes that served the national interest.
- If British banks were reluctant to fulfil this role, the process and purpose of an investment credit creation strategy could be undertaken by a national investment bank.

Agree an industrial strategy

- An effective economic policy based on the strategy of investment credit creation depends on the development of an agreed industrial strategy. This is seen as a prime requirement in other more successful economies.
- An effective industrial strategy for Britain would require agreement and support from government, industry and the banking sector. The task could be entrusted to a new Economic Planning Agency which would be responsible for bringing these elements together and advise government on implementing the new strategy.
- The strategy need not 'pick winners' but would establish criteria and measures of performance that would provide a context within which the normal processes for identifying worthwhile investment opportunities could operate.

Support affordable housing and reduce asset inflation

- While the new strategy would focus primarily on productive investment and employment, it could also be used for more specific purposes. It could, for example, be used to finance valuable infrastructure projects or to purchase enterprises that were important to the national interest, rather than allowing them to pass into foreign ownership. It could also be applied to purposes with a social focus.
- A deliberate use of credit creation to finance a house-building programme and reduce the price of housing would go a long way to resolving the UK's overvalued housing market, by establishing a much better balance between supply and demand and a substantial improvement in affordability.

● This is an example of how a macro-economic strategy that paid more attention to competitiveness and investment could directly target sources of inflation. Rather than ignoring the risk of inflation, it would enable policymakers to focus accurately on the real causes of inflationary pressures – in particular, housing – and to think more creatively and constructively about other options for dealing with them.

Introduce new goals for the economy

● An important benefit from a renewed debate about economic policy would be the possibility of replacing ideologically driven preoccupations – such as preserving the value of assets, reducing the size of government, and relying on austerity to escape recession – with goals that more accurately reflect the wider interest and represent a more comprehensive measure of economic success.
● The pamphlet recommends the following three key measures of success for the new economy:
    1. Full employment should be seen as the hallmark of a properly functioning economy.
    2. The fiscal deficit, while not necessarily the first priority, should indeed be reduced and eventually eliminated. But this should form part of a wider strategy to rebalance the economy rather than simply lower government expenditure.
    3. Inequality is widely recognized to reduce economic performance and so should be kept within reasonable limits.

In order to reflect these new goals, the Bank of England should be brought once again under democratic control. Its operating objectives should be redefined as the promotion of economic growth and full employment, and the control of inflation, within the guidelines of a national industrial plan.

Increase competitiveness

- The UK's lack of competitiveness and the consequent balance of payments constraint seem to preclude any lift in economic activity, such as might be brought about by the investment credit creation strategy advocated here. We should directly address our lack of competitiveness by the most obvious and effective means available: by bringing about a substantial devaluation of the currency.
- Our economic performance can be significantly improved and the current account constraint removed by a fall in the pound's value from its current level of about £1.00 = $1.40 to £1.00 = $1.10, with the same reduction applying against all currencies, a devaluation of about 21 per cent.
- A devaluation of this size would re-balance the UK economy towards manufacturing, investment and exports to the extent required to provide improvements in both the overall growth rate and the current account balance.

Bring the elements together

- The blind spot on competitiveness, and the dismissal of the real possibilities and true role of monetary policy and credit creation, are two of the major deficiencies in western, and particularly British, economic policy-making.
- What's more the two are directly linked: just as a tighter monetary policy will cause the exchange rate to rise, a looser monetary policy would cause the exchange rate to fall. Credit creation would itself encourage a devaluation because it would lead to lower interest rates.

● The combined strategy of providing increased funding for productive investment and encouraging that
investment through improving competitiveness therefore provides a coherent and credible economic strategy.
It would allow the left to offer a real choice to the voters
and enthuse those who are keen for change, without
departing in any way from mainstream economics.

INTRODUCTION

The election of Jeremy Corbyn to the Labour leadership owed much to his brave assertion that austerity is the wrong response to recession and that a successful economic policy should address the goals of improving our productive capacity and a fair distribution of the fruits of economic success.

Whether or not those assertions convince the wider electorate (and there is no reason why they should not), the mere fact that they have been made has changed the shape of the debate about both politics and economic policy. It has encouraged the growing emergence of a new mainstream consensus that at last offers a real alternative to neo-classical and 'free market' orthodoxy.

For those who welcome and support that development, however, there remain issues to be worked through. If we are to secure an economic future that relies on more than asset inflation and an unsustainable consumer boom, we first need a new approach to monetary policy so that the power of government can be used to stimulate much-needed investment in greater productive capacity and full employment. Second, any strategy for sustainable growth and increased investment will be frustrated unless the main inhibition to any policy for growth – the damaging and long-term loss of international competitiveness suffered by British industry – is overcome. This pamphlet addresses both of these central issues.

The main purpose of monetary policy has been seen for decades as simply the control of inflation. That function has been contracted out to the Bank of England and is accordingly beyond the reach of democratic accountability. Even in terms of this limited goal, however, it has created a major distortion. By far the greatest proportion of the money in our economy – estimated by the Bank of England at 97 per cent – is created by the commercial banks out of nothing, most of it lent out on mortgage, thereby encouraging asset inflation and consumption rather than productive investment. If it is acceptable for the banks to exercise this power for their own private purposes, why should the government not use it for wider public purposes?

The government's role in monetary policy, however, has been limited to the 'quantitative easing' (or, more pejoratively, 'printing money') that was undertaken as a panic response to the imminent collapse of the banking system following the global financial crisis. The willingness to take that action, however, surely raises the question as to why £375bn of new money can be safely provided for the purpose of bailing out the banks but should not even be contemplated for any other purpose.

Other countries, and at other times, have understood the great advantages of using monetary policy to provide investment finance for productive purposes; we should learn from their example. The post-war Japanese economic miracle, for example, was largely founded on an application of the Keynesian insight that new money provided for investment purposes cannot be inflationary if it is matched by a corresponding increase in output over an appropriate time scale.

Quantitative easing, appropriately directed to productive purposes in line with an agreed industrial strategy, would provide the stimulus and capacity for investment that British industry (whose current net investment level is approximately nil) desperately needs. But the demand for that investment finance is unlikely to materialise, for as long as British industry remains as uncompetitive as it has been for decades.

The evidence for that loss of competitiveness, while resolutely ignored by our policymakers, is unmistakable – a perennial trade deficit, a shrinking share of world markets including our own, a manufacturing industry that is struggling even to survive, let alone prosper, and the constant need to balance our payments by borrowing from overseas and selling our assets.

We hardly bother even to ask why this should be so. Yet the answers are staring us in the face. British industry is uncompetitive because we insist on charging more for our goods and services than the international market will bear. The most important determinant of international competitiveness is the exchange rate; it is the rate for sterling that translates all our domestic costs into international prices. At its current rate, it guarantees that British products are priced out of international markets.

Conventional wisdom tells us that the exchange rate is set by the market, but that is flatly contradicted by, among other things, the Japanese experience. A determined government can engineer a substantial devaluation (in the current Japanese case, by 48 per cent) if it takes appropriate action. That action, as in the Japanese case, will often take the form of an expansionary monetary policy and the government-authorised creation of new money.

The solutions to the two fundamental requirements of increased productive investment and improved competitiveness can therefore be seen as complementary. The policies required for one reinforce those needed for the other and make up a credible and coherent whole. A strategy built on these twin pillars would revolutionise our economic prospects.

1: A MONETARY POLICY FOR GROWTH

The central element of a coherent alternative to austerity is the provision of sufficient credit for investment purposes through a new approach to monetary policy – what Jeremy Corbyn and his advisers have called 'a people's quantitative easing'. Such a policy – conventionally dismissed as 'printing money' – has attracted attention because it is now more widely accepted that governments do indeed have – and on occasion use – the power to create new money. The only question is as to the purpose to which that new money is put.

One of the most difficult issues for the average person to grasp is that a country's economy operates quite differently from the economy of an individual person or company. One of the main reasons for this is the government's ability to create money. The individual or firm must accept that money has, at any given moment, a more or less fixed value. Similarly the quantity in the individual's hands will be limited by what they can earn, sell, borrow and so on. A government, however, can overcome a shortage of money by itself creating, or directing the banking system to create, more of it. There may well be consequences for governments that do so – consequences that are often regarded as undesirable – but it is increasingly recognised that governments do indeed have that power.

One of Keynes' most often quoted statements is that "there may be intrinsic reasons for the shortage of land but there are no intrinsic reasons for the shortage of capital." This undeniable truth is often obscured by governments' reluctance to acknowledge it, still less to be held to account for the positions they adopt on the issue. Indeed, many governments in the western world have adopted the current fashion of sub-contracting monetary policy to an 'independent' authority, usually the central bank or its governor or a committee responsible to the central bank.

The confusion has been compounded by the doctrine of monetarism, which maintains that the quantity of money must be held at a stable level in the interests of controlling inflation; indeed, it is argued that any other intervention by government would be ineffectual and beside the point.

Quantitative easing – government-created money

The global financial crisis was so terrifying in its threat of financial meltdown followed by disastrous recession that a number of western governments abandoned their ideological preferences in favour of emergency action. That action comprised a deliberate policy of 'printing money' in a desperate attempt to ward off a crisis of illiquidity as the banking system threatened to implode.

In the US, the Federal Reserve pumped trillions of dollars into the US economy, at a rate as high as $85bn per month; the result has been that the Federal Reserve's assets have more than quadrupled to upwards of $4tn. Some of that money has undoubtedly helped to increase the pace of recovery, and even to make some impression on unemployment. However, much of it has found its way more or less directly into the accounts of banks and other major corporations and thence into stock markets, which have accordingly enjoyed a substantial boom.

The UK government, too, undertook a programme of printing money, though on a smaller scale; the programme aimed at a total of £375bn. There have, of course, been earlier instances of this practice, even if it was usually done surreptitiously. I recall that in the late 1970s, Jim Callaghan's government indulged on occasion in what was then called 'overfunding'; that is, writing cheques to itself for more than was actually due. This phenomenon was hardly identified, let alone commented upon at the time, so cautiously was it done.

The role of the banks

What is really astonishing about the conventional position is that the insistence that government's prime duty is to maintain a stable quantity of money is, in fact, a charade. Governments have not only turned a blind eye to massive increases in the money supply but have actually sub-contracted the power to create money to private companies who use the power to make large profits at the expense of the rest of the economy. Those private companies are of course banks.

The truth of this matter is gradually becoming accepted, albeit with a fierce and stubborn rearguard action by those who choose not to recognise it. A significant milestone was achieved in the first quarter of 2014 with the publication of an important paper in the Bank of England *Quarterly Bulletin*.[1] In that paper, three Bank of England economists acknowledged that overwhelmingly the greatest proportion of money in the economy – they estimate that it amounts to 97 per cent – is created by the banks out of nothing.

Most people will tell you that the banks lend out to borrowers the money that is deposited with them by savers; they are simply intermediaries which charge for the service they provide in bringing savers and borrowers together. The truth, however, now conceded by the central bank, is very different. When a bank lends you money, it simply makes a book entry that credits you with an agreed sum; that sum represents nothing but the bank's willingness to lend. The debt you thereby owe the bank does not represent in any sense money that was actually deposited with the bank or the capital held by the bank. The money that banks lend has very little to do with the savings deposited with them and is many times greater than their total. As John Kenneth Galbraith said in 1976: "The process by which banks create money is so simple that the mind is repelled".[2]

There are of course many who scoff at the proposition that banks create money out of nothing. If they could do so, the argument goes, why would any bank ever go bankrupt? But, as the Bank of England paper points out, when bank loans on a mortgage are repaid, they cease to be money. They are no longer available to the borrowers and they are no longer assets in the bank's books. That is why banks cannot just create money for their own use; the money they create is available only to the borrower. The banks make their profits not by writing cheques to themselves but by charging interest on the money they create to lend to others.

But, for the lifetime of those loans (which could be decades), they will have added to the money supply and to the spending power enjoyed by the borrower. And by the time the loans are repaid, they will have been replaced many times over by new loans created for new borrowers over years, if not decades and generations. It is no accident that there is a strong correlation between new bank lending and growth in the money supply.

There will, in the search for the ever higher bank profits, always be the temptation to lend more than is prudent for their own interests or desirable in the wider interest. And the consequent huge increase in private sector debt was, as we know, a major contributing factor in the development of the global financial crisis. What's more, it is bank-created credit that provides the major stimulus to asset inflation in the housing market, with all of its deleterious economic and social costs, which at the same time diverts essential investment capital away from where it is really needed: the productive sector of the economy.

The banks and housing

The banks give priority to lending for house purchase since it requires by far the least effort, and is the most secure and profitable form of lending – and there is virtually never any shortage of willing borrowers. Experience over decades has taught homeowners that the value of their homes, unlike any other asset of remotely comparable value, will go on rising over time. In buying a house, they not only gain necessary accommodation, but also an appreciating capital asset. No other asset of comparable value and of such significance to the economy as a whole is traded in a market where its value goes on rising by virtue of the new money constantly created for the very purpose of investing in it.

This process really built up a head of steam when banks moved in to replace much more conservative building societies and to dominate the mortgage market in the 1980s. It has meant that, over a generation or two, there has been a constant injection of new mortgage finance (at a much faster rate than the growth of incomes or of most other asset values) into the housing market. That constant process underpins and reinforces the already inflated value brought about by earlier mortgage lending and is steadily and cumulatively built into the rising market prices of our houses, and of the land on which they are built.

Homeowners who see the value of their properties rising fast are encouraged by the increase in the value of their equity, whether or not immediately realised, to feel better off and therefore more able to spend and consume more freely, constituting a major reflationary impulse in the British economy. But this is of course more than a purely economic outcome. Because only those who already have a foothold in the market, or who otherwise have substantial assets and income, can participate, the inflated housing market operates as a giant mechanism that continually transfers wealth to asset-holders – homeowners – and away from those who do not own their homes.

Responses to orthodoxy

As the truth about how most of our money is created becomes better known and more widely accepted, a wide range of responses to that new perception is developing. Many commentators advocate what can variously be described as full or 100 per cent reserve banking,[3] limited purpose banking,[4] or positive money.[5] Proposals such as these, which have been endorsed by Martin Wolf in the *Financial Times*,[6] have in common the notion that private lending should be limited to pre-existing money – a contention that would put an end to the banks' power of credit creation. It can be traced back to Irving Fisher and the 'Chicago plan' of the 1930s, which later won the support of, among others, Milton Friedman.[7]

Among the most interesting proponents of a more radical response to the truth about credit creation, however, are a group of economists who have called their views the 'modern monetary theory' (MMT). They take the position that, as Joe Guinan says, "the notion of a revenue-constrained government budget in a monetarily sovereign state may be a useful fiction for conservatives and rentier capitalists, but it should not have gone unchallenged".[8] Among the leading proponents of this broad approach are L. Randall Wray and

Stephanie Kelton of the University of Missouri–Kansas City, Pavlina Tcherneva, and Victoria Chick. MMT also enjoys qualified support in the UK from such post-Keynesian economists as Steve Keen and Ann Pettifor.

This group of economists is ready to ask fundamental questions. If a monetarily sovereign state can create all the money it needs, then why tax at all? Quite simply, as L. Randall Wray explains, there is 'no longer any balance sheet operation in which government "spends" its tax revenues'.[9] And, as Ann Pettifor has argued, echoing Keynes, 'we can afford what we can do'.[10]

Some proponents of MMT advocate what Keynes called direct job creation, where government acts as the employer of last resort.[11] Keynes himself was clear that simply increasing public spending, and financing that by borrowing, would not necessarily do what was required to lift effective demand and bring about full employment.

Even when the economy was operating at or near full capacity, effective demand might still be too low to provide jobs for those who would be the least likely to find work, and that problem would of course become more difficult and sizeable in times of recession. In these circumstances, pump-priming in the usual sense might be diverted to purposes such as debt repayment or capital investment or higher prices that might do little to raise effective demand. What's more, borrowing to increase public spending might merely transfer resources from one part of the economy to another, and the private sector could not be expected to go beyond its own interests in lifting the demand for labour. Keynes' response was therefore to require the government (or the public sector on the government's behalf) to be the employer of last resort and to offer jobs to all those available for work.

However, MMT and direct job creation do not, in their pure form, look like practical politics in any foreseeable future. The conventional objection is that they would tempt governments to spend without limit. There would be huge (though not necessarily rational) resistance from employers who would fear the consequences for wage levels in general of full employment at a level that meant that everyone who wanted to work would have a job. And if the government is to take such a central role, the corollary would seem to be that there would be no need to involve the banks in credit creation. It may not be wise or necessary to take on the whole world of finance at once in this way.

Moreover, while direct job creation would undoubtedly provide a virtual guarantee of full employment which would be hugely valuable, it would not necessarily achieve all that we might seek from a properly functioning economic policy. While full employment would do something to lift the level of effective demand, it would not directly provide to the productive sector, either public or private, the kind of investment finance that is available in other more successful economies.

A modification of the pure MMT position would allow the banks to continue to create credit but limit and direct the purposes to which that new money could be put. This approach would restore the money-creating power to the government, with the banks acting as the government's agents.[12] This might well be described as a 'people's quantitative easing'; it would, however, be used not just as a remedy for recession but as a deliberate attempt to launch a failing economy into a new orbit. It has, as we shall see, enjoyed success when applied elsewhere and at other times, and objections, whether theoretical or practical, seem hard to sustain in the light of what we now know about quantitative easing and credit creation by the banks.

2: THE PURPOSES OF CREDIT CREATION

The current orthodoxy concerning the scope and purpose of monetary policy has meant that a potentially powerful instrument in the hands of government has been given up or misapplied. The overlooked but centrally important function of monetary policy is to encourage the long-established propensity of a market economy to grow; that is, to increase output. We could not have achieved our current standard of living without it.

Monetarism, looking as it does at only one side of the supply and demand equation, gives insufficient weight to that propensity. This is surprising when one considers that the proponents of monetarism claim to be the most committed supporters of the 'free' market. An inappropriate, and particularly an inadequate, money supply can inhibit expansion, as we shall see later from the Japanese experience over the two decades 1990 to 2010. Keynes was well aware of the important potential of credit creation and recognised that, as a central element in macroeconomic policy when properly deployed, it can and does serve a much wider range of purposes than the current focus on house purchase and speculative financial transactions.

It could be used, for example, to raise purchasing power by putting more money in people's pockets, and can thereby help to resolve a problem of deficient demand. Or, it could be used to 'monetise the debt' – a painless way to reduce the government's deficit by a calculated amount. Such a policy is often pejoratively characterised as 'helicopter money' – the notion that demand could be raised if pound notes were scattered from the air – but has been seriously analysed by reputable economists such as Adair Turner and Michael Woodford who have reached the point of debating whether it would best be delivered by fiscal measures (such as tax cuts) or by monetary policy (essentially printing money).[13]

Credit creation has also been used, as we know, to stabilise the financial system. This is the quantitative easing that over recent times has been implemented by governments in both the UK and the US, and now the European Union as well, to remedy the precarious situation of an otherwise bankrupt financial system in the wake of the global financial crisis.

Credit creation can also be used to fund large-scale projects that are vitally important to the economy but are too large or not commercially rewarding enough to attract private capital. It offers an alternative to borrowing as a source of funding, though there is, in light of the current low rate at which the government can borrow, no reason why borrowing should not be made for public infrastructure purposes. Indeed this is a sensible and cheaper alternative to the public/private partnerships that are currently preferred for ideological reasons.

There is a case, depending on the precise circumstances, for each of these uses of credit creation. The most interesting and important form of credit creation in our current circumstances, however, is targeted at increasing investment in productive industry, with the goal of increasing productivity, accelerating the rate of economic growth and providing full employment.

This type of credit creation may be called investment credit creation. In the countries where it is practised, it is usually delivered through the trading banks at the behest of the central bank and the government. It is supported by Keynes' perceptive assertion that there is no reason why the provision of credit for the purpose of productive investment should not precede the increase in output that it is intended to produce, provided that the increase occurs over an appropriate time frame. The proviso is of course important, as we shall see when looking at the Japanese and Chinese experience, and requires that investment credit creation should be carefully directed and calibrated. Other economies have understood and benefited from this insight and have used investment credit creation to stimulate growth, without being inhibited by the conviction that any increase in the money supply must necessarily be inflationary.

There are excellent precedents for this approach to monetary policy. In the US, President Roosevelt, foreseeing correctly that the US would be drawn into the second world war, used the two years before Pearl Harbour to provide virtually unlimited capital, through credit creation – that is, simply by printing money – to American industry, so that the country could rapidly increase its military capability. Roosevelt encountered the usual objections from conventional economists but the exigencies of war and his own political strength and will prevailed. The results of this quite deliberate strategy were spectacular and hugely significant. American industrial output grew by an unprecedented 12.2% per annum from 1938 to 1944 – an outcome that went a long way towards enabling the US, and the Allies more generally, to win the second world war.

A second example occurred in the post-war period when, crippled by defeat and nuclear bombing, Japanese industry was enabled by similar means to grow at a rapid rate as part of a similarly deliberate policy. This was advanced by Osamu Shimomura, a Keynesian economist who – while virtually unknown in the west – had understood the Keynesian message that credit creation for the purposes of investment in new productive capacity could be non-inflationary, provided that the new capacity duly did materialise over an appropriate time scale so that the increased output matched the increased money supply. The outcome of Shimomuran economics was so successful that in a matter of just two decades, Japan advanced from being a shattered and defeated enemy to dominate the world market for mass-produced manufactured goods.

An equally important and revealing example of investment credit creation and of an economy enjoying rapid economic growth without complying with the prescriptions of neo-classical free-market economics can be seen in today's China. There, similar Shimomuran techniques – no doubt learned from the Japanese experience – have been used to finance the rapid expansion of Chinese manufacturing. The Chinese central bank, under instructions from the government, makes credit available to Chinese enterprises that can demonstrate their ability to comply with the government's economic priorities in the course of building or buying new capacity.

The irony of this is that when Chinese interests buy strategic assets in western economies, as they increasingly do, the money will often come from credit created by the People's Bank of China out of nothing. There is no reason in principle why western banks could not have fulfilled that purpose.

The Japanese experience

The post-war Japanese experience is particularly instructive as to how investment credit creation works. Adopting the Keynesian view that investment is the major key to economic development, Osamu Shimomura showed that an economy could increase its investment level through credit created at the central bank, provided that the credit was earmarked for commercial and industrial investment. The rapidity of Japanese industrial development in the 1960s and 1970s, in response to the stimulus provided by investment credit creation by the Bank of Japan under instructions from the government, is widely seen in Asian economies as a vindication of Shimomuran policies.[14]

Professor Kenneth K Kurihara (1910–1972) was one of the most influential interpreters of Shimomuran economics; he had the great advantage (from a western viewpoint) of being able to write in English. He concluded his analysis of Shimomuran policies with the following summary:

"If, therefore, greater investment can be financed partly by credits, there is no need for that 'abstinence' which the classical economists considered necessary for economic progress, any more than there is for that 'austerity' which some present day underdeveloped countries impose on already under-consuming populations at the constant peril of social unrest. Nor is it difficult, in such credit-creating circumstances, to agree with Keynes' observation that investment and consumption should be regarded as complementary rather than competitive."[15]

The Japanese slowdown in the early 1990s occurred only when the Bank of Japan abandoned its focus on productive investment, and credit creation was applied increasingly to speculative purposes. This brought about, as it has regularly done in the west, an asset bubble (at one point, Japanese property prices were so high that Japanese land – at only 4 per cent of the area of the US – was valued at four times as much as the worth of all US property). When the bubble burst, many assets were revealed not to possess their supposed value, bad debts soared, and the increase in the volume of money that had stimulated the Japanese economy over three decades was suddenly thrown into reverse.

In the wake of the stagnation that followed, Japan was persuaded by western (and largely American) economists from the IMF and the World Bank to adopt the newly dominant principles of neo-classical economics which had recently captured western economies. This significant change in policy allows us to subject different policy settings to the real test of practical outcomes.

In doing so, we have the great advantage of detailed work carried out by Professor Richard Werner who became the first Shimomura Fellow at the Research Institute for Capital Formation at the Development Bank of Japan where he spent 10 years in the 1990s and was able to observe at close quarters the onset of the economic stagnation of Japan over this period.

In his *New Paradigm in Macroeconomics*,[16] Werner considers which of the conventional explanations usually offered might actually correlate with the observable outcomes over that period. He surveys in turn a range of factors, including fiscal policy, interest rates, the supposed need postulated by the IMF for "structural change" (or neo-liberal policies), and the significance of changes (in both directions) of asset prices and capital flows.

What he found was that none of the conventional accounts were able to explain – in the sense of showing a significant correlation with – the observable performance of the Japanese economy over the period of its stagnation from 1990 onwards. The neo-classical insistence that reducing interest rates would stimulate economic growth was given an extended test, with short-term interest rates cut to a negligible 0.001 per cent by 2004. Fiscal stimulation, totalling well over 120tn yen was tried and central government debt rose accordingly to 150 per cent of GDP by 2002, but this simply moved resources and debt from one part of the economy – the private sector – to another – the public sector.

The finger was then pointed at 'supply-side' constraints; capital markets were accordingly 'liberalised', cartels were broken up, the banking system allowed the greater inflow of foreign capital, minimal government intervention was insisted upon, and monetary policy eventually became the exclusive prerogative of an independent Bank of Japan. But the correlation between 'structural reform' and a resumption of economic growth was precisely nil.

The one area that escaped scrutiny was the operation of the banking system. As stagnation proved resistant to the conventional remedies, however, it began to occur to a few economists that the 'credit crunch' that had occurred both in the US and Japan in the early years of the decade might conceivably have something to do with it. Werner argues that this is indeed the only credible explanation – though he leaves out of consideration the correlative impact of monetary policy on the exchange rate which appreciated strongly over the period in question and undoubtedly also had a deflationary impact.

On the rare occasions that western economists have been invited to consider the issue, they have maintained that correlation is not causation, and that there is no evidence that the new credit created by the Bank of Japan 'caused' the observed growth in the 1960s and 1970s, or that the cessation of that growth was the consequence of abandoning credit creation for productive investment purposes. And because Werner's work related specifically to the Japanese economy, there was a temptation to treat his conclusions as having no wider application to western economies.

It is, however, very hard to dismiss Werner's conclusions so easily. He applied Granger predictive causation analysis – developed by Nobel Prize-winning British economist Sir Clive Granger – which allows it to be shown whether there is a predictive link between two items of economic time series. He was able to show that there is a clear Granger causation predictive link between the rate of investment credit creation at the Bank of Japan and subsequent rates of Japanese economic growth, both positive and negative.

The downside risk

The Japanese experience over recent decades shows, however, that investment credit creation is not a free pass to economic success. It tells us that credit created for investment must be just that; it must be directed accurately and carefully to productive purposes and can be justified only where, as Keynes argued, it stimulates increased output that will match the increase in the money supply.

We can now see evidence that China is entering a similarly dangerous phase. While official figures show that the Chinese economy continues to grow strongly (albeit – at just under 7 per cent per annum – more slowly), it is increasingly clear that bank lending for construction in the housing market has left the Chinese banking system over-extended. There is a huge glut of unsold houses not only leaving the banks with assets of little immediate value to match their lending, but saddling the wider economy with superfluous infrastructure projects and with an expected stimulus to consumption from sustained demand for new household equipment to put in the new houses failing to materialise.

It remains to be seen, however, whether China can be more successful than Japan was in managing the overhang of potentially bad debts and the transition to a more restrained model of credit creation; it may be that avoiding Japan's difficulties will require that China accepts a slower rate of growth than has become the norm.

Investment credit creation in the UK

The objection that will immediately be raised to adopting a Japanese-style approach through investment credit creation in the UK is that it would, in accordance with monetarist theory, be inflationary – though no explanation is offered as to why that should be so in the case of the UK when it is not in others. The Bank of England has of course already undertaken quantitative easing on a significant scale, and this has had no discernible influence on inflation; there is no reason why that should have been any different if some or all of that increase in the money supply had been diverted away from bank balance sheets and to productive investment. And, as we have seen, the current orthodoxy is completely relaxed about the huge increases in the money supply brought about by the banks for the purposes of lending for house purchase.

The objection will also be made that the UK is not a developing economy, as Japan and China were, and that a monetary expansion in a developed economy would be fraught with danger. But this did not seem to be a problem for FDR's pre-war United States, and the UK's current lack of competitiveness, diminished manufacturing capacity, pitiful rate of investment and falling share of word trade mean that we are best regarded as in need of development – that is, a (hopefully) developing rather than developed economy.

It is important to grasp that this condition of stunted development means that the productive capacity of the UK economy is far from being optimised and needs to be unlocked. An expansion in the money supply could be inflationary only when the economy is already fully utilising its productive capacity (and even then – and importantly – an expanded money supply could well re-define upwards that productive capacity).

The notion that monetary policy might be adapted to serve the goal of expansion is, at least in some quarters, no longer seen as fanciful. Leading monetary economists like Adair Turner[17] and Michael Woodford debate which precise mechanisms of both fiscal and monetary policy would be most effective in extending the monetary base and thereby raising the level of economic activity. They recognise that the quantitative easing practised so far has failed to focus on this most desirable outcome.

To sum up, investment credit creation would benefit the economy both directly and indirectly. Directly, because of the increased money made available for investment in productive capacity and indirectly, because the productive economy would be spared the anti-growth measures, such as high interest rates and an overvalued currency, that are seen as necessary to restrain the inflationary effects of credit creation when it is used, as at present, for speculative purposes.

3: PRODUCTIVE INVESTMENT

Most economists are agreed that any strategy for improving the UK's economic performance must address the distressingly low rate of investment by comparison with more successful economies that has long been a feature of the UK economy. As with the balance of payments deficit, it is such a long-standing phenomenon that, while occasionally deplored, it is simply accepted as part of the natural order. Even when it is recognised, the remedies offered by current orthodoxy are in short supply. With the return on productive investment as low as it is, there can be little surprise that the new money created through bank-created credit goes anywhere but into new productive capacity.

It is nevertheless surprising and shocking to realise just how dismal the UK performance is. Capital investment as a percentage of UK GDP continues to fall and, at 14 per cent, places the UK at the 142nd ranking out of 154 economies surveyed, equal with El Salvador. The world average is 23.8 per cent; the figure for China is 46.1 per cent.

Even these figures do not tell the whole story. Capital consumption runs at about 11.5 per cent per annum, leaving a net investment figure of just 2.5 per cent. Even that meagre figure has to be adjusted to take account of a growing total population, so that net investment per head is approximately nil. At this level, without any real increase in net investment, it is impossible to see any prospect of industrial regeneration in the UK economy.

A new focus for the banking system

A strategy that selectively applied credit creation to productive purposes could be used in a number of ways but its principal purpose would be the provision of cost-free or at least low-cost credit to productive industry. This would be aimed at lifting the rate of investment in new technology, product development and marketing skills, and the employment and training of staff and workforces to help raise output and productivity.

The most effective way of doing this would be to utilise the existing range of banking services but to ensure that they functioned and re-focused under the direction of the central bank and for purposes that served the national interest. It was this process of credit creation for productive purposes by the banking system – following what was called 'window guidance' from the Bank of Japan, and in line with the industrial strategy developed by the government – that underpinned Japan's rapid development. Prime minister Shinzo Abe has now re-introduced these policies, specifically referring to them as 'Shimomuran' – though their beneficial impact has been blunted by the simultaneous raising of the rates of indirect taxation.

If a similar process is to succeed in the UK, the banking system would need to reform and re-focus. One of the principal reasons for our low level of investment has been the absence of a supportive financial-industrial banking system in the United Kingdom. A more effective banking system that would help to finance much-needed investment in new productive capacity is clearly needed.

British banks are characterised by the low level of their lending to business. They claim that this does not evidence any reluctance to do so, but merely a shortage of demand – or, to put it another way, a shortage of suitable projects on which to lend. But no sense of this can be made unless we know the terms on which the banks are offering to lend.

The information that is available shows that, by comparison with other and more successful economies, our banks lend over a shorter term. Repayment, in other words, has to be made faster. This means that the annual repayment costs of bank loans for British firms over the life of the loan are much higher, the adverse impact on cash-flow is therefore more severe, and the need to make an immediate return on investment (and a quick boost to profitability) is much greater.

A large part of the reason for the greater amount and ease of bank borrowing enjoyed by businesses in, for example, Germany and Japan, and in the new powerhouses of China, Korea and Taiwan, is the fact that their annual repayment costs are substantially lower than in Britain. This is, of course, why they are so often able to buy up and make a profit from our failing assets.

Short-term cash-flow or liquidity is at least as important to British firms as longer-term profitability; indeed, it can be a matter of life and death. It is a factor that both inhibits the willingness to borrow (thereby reducing access to essential investment capital) in the first place, and – if the loan is made – greatly increases the chances that it cannot be repaid in accordance with the loan period and the terms insisted upon by the banks.

If, as is all too likely, a business borrowing on these terms runs into difficulties before the return on the investment funded by the borrowing becomes available, the news gets worse. British banks, unlike their overseas counterparts, show little interest in the survival of their customers. Their sole concern is to recover the loan and interest payments due to them over the short period specified in the loan arrangement.

While the secondary finance market plays a role, the greater part of lending in the UK is undertaken by just six major trading banks. By contrast, the more successful German economy has seven regional banks, 431 Sparkassen (or local savings banks) and a network of 15,600 branches to provide small and medium sized enterprise (SME) loans to local businesses. Each Sparkassen concentrates on providing business loans to SMEs in the area where it is located, and each has an interest in, and commitment to, ensuring the economic success of its village, city or region.

We need, in other words, a banking system that provides proper security and guarantees to savers, that truly serves the public interest and that in particular provides much-needed investment finance to SMEs. Such a system would replicate many of the advantages provided to their respective economies by the banking systems in countries like Germany and Japan. If, for any reason, British banks showed reluctance to fulfil this role, it would be necessary to return to the concept of a national investment bank to ensure that the process and purpose of an investment credit creation strategy was undertaken.

An agreed industrial strategy

An effective economic policy based on the strategy of investment credit creation will, however, depend for its effectiveness on a further element: the development of an agreed industrial strategy. The development of such a strategy is seen as a prime requirement in other more successful economies. It is an obvious feature of a centrally directed economy such as China, and is equally seen as a necessity by many other countries; it has been adopted in wartime by the US and the UK. Other democratic countries with market economies, such as Japan, have found that some kind of industrial planning is required as the basis for policy and action.

In the west, however, deliberate and coordinated economic planning seems out of tune with the current obeisance to unfettered market forces. This does not mean, however, that a country like the UK should find the development of an industrial strategy difficult or objectionable in principle when the practical advantages are not only obvious but cannot be overlooked.

An effective industrial strategy for Britain would require agreement and support from each of government, industry (both employers and workforces) and the banking sector. The task could be entrusted to a new Economic Planning Agency which would be responsible for bringing these elements together and for providing competent, timely and accurate advice to the government on how best to implement the new strategy.

The strategy need not 'pick winners' in detail or operate in too prescriptive a manner but would establish criteria and measures of performance that would provide a context within which the normal processes for identifying worthwhile investment opportunities could operate. In this way, a great deal of the decision-making could be left to the usual agencies, providing that they operated within the agreed strategy.

Affordable housing and asset inflation

While the new strategy would focus primarily on productive investment and employment, it could also be used for more specific purposes. It could, for example, be used to finance valuable infrastructure projects or to purchase enterprises that were important to the national interest, rather than allowing them to pass into foreign ownership – particularly when the foreign buyers were using credit created for them by their own banking sectors. But it could also be applied to purposes with a social focus.

An OECD report[18] last year described housing in the UK as overvalued and with prices still rising. A deliberate use of credit creation to finance a house-building programme and reduce the price of housing would go a long way to resolving this problem, by establishing a much better balance between supply and demand and a substantial improvement in affordability.

A government prepared to finance such a programme could do so either by creating the necessary finance directly, by buying housing assets directly or by investing in companies prepared to create such assets. They could do this secure in the knowledge that its investment would cost little and would be matched by an increase in assets and helped by a rise in tax revenues. More conventionally, government could issue housing bonds specifically designed to finance house construction.

Inflation

The corollary of investment credit creation would be more effective regulation of the bank lending currently provided for house purchase. This is not exactly a novel idea; there is a growing recognition that to allow the banks the unrestrained freedom to go on lending for house purchase is to invite a full re-run of the global financial crisis.

In New Zealand, for example, the Reserve Bank has already implemented a restriction on bank lending in the form of a loan-to-value ratio and this is likely to be the precursor of similar and more ambitious and widely applicable measures. The Bank of England's Financial Policy Committee recommended a similar policy in June 2014, requiring that lenders should limit to 15 per cent the proportion of new mortgages at loan-to-income multiples of 4.5 or more.[19] The UK government announced in February 2015 that it would give the Bank of England the power to enforce such a recommendation.

There is of course precedent for such an approach. Before the Thatcher government released the banks from all controls other than interest rates in 1980, the central bank was much readier to use loan-to-value ratios and other similar measures (generally referred to as "the corset") to restrain bank lending.

Such policies are usually described as 'macro-prudential' measures but are attracting attention for their macro-economic significance rather than their prudential impact. It is gradually dawning on our central bankers that the interest rate instrument is more ineffectual than they had believed – that it scarcely operates as a restraint on the bankers' continuing incentive to lend, which in turn is does considerable damage to, and creates major risks for, the economy as a whole.

We may conclude that a macro-economic strategy that paid more attention to competitiveness and expansion does not imply a failure or refusal to address inflation effectively. It would on the contrary free up policymakers to focus more accurately on the real causes of inflationary pressures and to think more creatively and constructively about other options for dealing with them. We might even accept that, in a growing economy, a regulated and reasonable inflation rate is a valuable incentive to innovation, a lubricant of change and the hallmark of an economy that is functioning well. And inflation, after all, occurs when the money supply increases faster than the increase in real output; it is time we stopped looking exclusively at the money supply and paid more attention to the output side of the equation.

An important benefit from a renewed debate about economic policy would be the possibility of replacing ideologically driven preoccupations, such as preserving the value of assets, reducing the size of government, and relying on austerity to escape recession, with goals that more accurately reflect the wider interest and represent a more comprehensive measure of economic success. Prime amongst such goals would be full employment.

Full employment is of course an elusive concept, particularly after decades of manipulating statistics, re-classifying the jobless, wages at less than a living-wage level, and ignoring those who would join the job market or work full-time rather than part-time if they saw any prospect of full-time and properly paid employment. But full employment, almost however defined, as the central goal of policy would not only be the most important step that could be taken to relieve poverty and to reverse the destructive growth in inequality; it would also be a huge step towards a more inclusive and therefore more successful economy. There is nothing economically efficient about keeping large numbers out of work and unwillingly dependent on benefits.

Full employment should be seen as the hallmark of a properly functioning economy. An economy that is competitive in the sense that it can find profitable markets for what it produces, and for which investment capital is available to finance increased production, should be able to use the productive capacity of its total workforce. Conversely, a high or persistent rate of unemployment shows that those conditions do not apply. Once it is accepted that full employment is both desirable and achievable, the success or otherwise of economic policy would be judged according to a criterion that was easily understood by the public.

The government deficit

The austerity measures that are said to be necessary to eliminate the government deficit have been notably ineffective in doing so. The cuts in government spending that have been thought necessary in the long and painful struggle to bring the economy back to its 2007 level have meant that tax revenues have been lower and that the costs of unemployment have been higher than they might otherwise have been. This implies a protracted government deficit and consequentially rising debt hanging over us for years to come. With growth slowing, more cuts promised, and reductions in the deficit stalling, with the deficit likely to continue at around its present level, total government debt will continue to grow and could well approach 100 per cent of GDP.

Let us accept, however, that a reduction and eventual elimination of the government's deficit, while not necessarily the first priority, is a sensible and achievable goal. Even then, it is surely better addressed as part of a wider strategy. If we set aside the political motivations for wishing to see lower government expenditure, the best way of reducing the deficit – even in conventional terms – would be to locate it in a more buoyant economy. In such an economy, tax revenues would rise, and the costs of unemployment and all its attendant social ills would be much reduced. Government spending, even if it remained constant in total, would fall as a proportion of the economy as the economy grew larger.

The priority given to the government's deficit looks even more misplaced when one considers the even more protracted balance of payments deficit and the fact that the two deficits are closely linked. The current account deficit amounts to the sum of the deficits incurred by the government and the private sector (that is, households and the corporate sector combined); they are accounting identities. If the current account deficit remains unaddressed, the only way that the government's deficit can be reduced is if the private sector develops an even larger deficit of its own. The strategy advocated here would rebalance the economy, so that both the current account deficit and the government's deficit would reduce and eventually disappear.

The direction of government spending, rather than intensifying the contractionary forces in the economy, could then play its full and proper part as an essential factor in a healthy and properly functioning economy. This would not mean a free-for-all in public spending; it would still be necessary to ensure that the spending secured value for money and was properly monitored and accounted for. But it would put an end to an economically destructive and politically prejudiced animus against public spending per se.

Inequality

Many commentators have observed that a disappointing economic performance has often been accompanied by a widening inequality; indeed, international statistics, and recent OECD reports, suggest that the two go hand in hand. Those countries with higher levels of inequality, like the US and the UK, have performed worse in economic terms than those, like Germany, Japan, Korea and the Scandinavian countries, where inequality has been kept within reasonable limits.

The debate about inequality has, however, been galvanised by the recent publication of *Capital in the Twenty-First Century* by Thomas Piketty. Piketty has analysed a huge volume of data – going back for a couple of centuries or more – to support his conclusion that the natural operation of capitalism is to produce a greater and greater degree of inequality. That conclusion seems justified by the experience of the past three or four decades, when almost the whole of the increase in wealth in western countries has gone to the richest tier of the population, and the share of the national income accounted for by profits has risen while the share of wages has fallen.[20]

Piketty has done an excellent job in providing historical and comparative evidence to show the virtual universality of this tendency. But he has done no more in reality than to confirm through statistical analysis the conclusions that many others have reached through common sense and careful observation. He supports, in particular, the conclusion reached by Joseph Stiglitz, that the incomes of the rich in today's economy are usually those of the rentier – that is, they are returns on existing capital – rather than those of the job creator and investor in new wealth-creating capacity of current mythology.

The important part of Piketty's work, however, lies in his assertion that these outcomes are the inevitable features of a capitalist economy. He shows that the growing divide between rich and poor arises because the return on capital automatically (not of course in every case, but as a general proposition) grows faster than the rate of growth of the economy as a whole (though some commentators have begun to ask, in the light of recent declines in rates of return in western economies, whether that state of affairs might be about to change).

He goes on to argue that this is the way it has always been, with few exceptions, since the dawn of capitalism, and he predicts that the pace of this widening of inequality is about to speed up. The greater the concentration of wealth, in other words, the more rapidly those few who control it will use it to extend their advantage.

Piketty's thesis points us in a further direction, however. He acknowledges that, especially in the immediate post-war period and particularly in countries like the UK, the share of income and wealth of the richest fell by comparison with the rest of society. He explains this by pointing out that the second world war had destroyed or decimated the value of many of the assets – both physical and financial – previously owned by the rich, so that their capital base was much reduced.

But he also acknowledges that there were other factors at work – many of them political rather than strictly economic, and designed rather than accidental. The war had necessarily, by requiring a combined effort from all parts of society, reduced social divisions; working people, and women in particular, had learnt to have more confidence in their abilities and in the value of their contribution. They were determined to learn the lessons of the period after the first world war when the interests of working people had been sacrificed on the altar of the gold standard.

When the voters rejected Winston Churchill and his Conservatives in favour of a relatively untested Labour government, there can have been no more dramatic evidence of the determination of the people who had won the war that democracy would make a real difference. The result was a drive to increase taxation on the wealthy (and on their unearned income from capital as well as on their high salaries), to increase the rights of working people at work through strong trade unions, to improve the services available to ordinary people through major initiatives like the

National Health Service, and to place the government's responsibility for the maintenance of full employment at the centre of economic policy.

What this demonstrates is that, if we want a society that is more equal and an economy that is more efficient in utilising all of its resources, and especially its human resources, then political intervention in the market process is absolutely required. To put it simply, the gap between rich and poor can be prevented from widening by ensuring that the economy as a whole grows faster than the net return on capital.

Restoring macro-economic policy to democratic control

The elevation of a supposedly 'independent' central bank to the role of unchallengeable arbiter of macro-economic policy was widely applauded when Gordon Brown, following New Zealand's example, introduced it in the UK in 1997. It can hardly be argued that it has produced successful results, but it is still virtually never questioned.

The notion that a central bank should be independent was hardly a new one, and no one – until very recently – had ever thought that it had any particular merit. Concepts of what independence might mean, as in the case of the Federal Reserve of the United States, have varied considerably over the years. Both the Radcliffe Committee and the Wilson Committee in the United Kingdom rejected greater independence for the Bank of England. Others have noted that independence is likely to result in the poor coordination of monetary and fiscal policy, or at the very least in the primacy of monetary over fiscal policy.

So how has central bank independence come to be seen as the essential guarantor of economic virtue? It is not as though the record shows that independence has achieved anything of great value. As James Forder has shown,[21] much of the belief that independence has produced worthwhile outcomes in terms of policy stability and control of inflation rests on mere assertion and a partisan interpretation of the evidence.

The evidence is that handing monetary policy over to the tender care of a central bank is simply a reinforcement of the current and increasingly discredited orthodoxy that inflation should be the only concern and focus of monetary policy and macro-economic policy more generally; and that its treatment is simply a technical matter that is properly the preserve of unaccountable bankers, and is not to be trusted to unreliable politicians. Quite apart from the undemocratic nature of this approach, whereby what are said to be the most important decisions in economic policy-making are removed from the democratic arena, we have paid a heavy economic price for allowing the bankers' interest to prevail over the interests of the economy as a whole.

It has suited the politicians well to be able to disclaim any responsibility for policies (and their consequences) for which they are ultimately responsible. What's more, it was the ability to disclaim responsibility for monetary policy by handing it over to a European central bank that was always one of the (usually unstated) supposed advantages of joining the euro.

This very issue was succinctly discussed, as it happens, by members of the Japanese Committee on Financial System Research (Kinyu Seido Chosa Kai) as it considered whether to revise the 1942 Japan Law that established the Bank of Japan's primary objective as the promotion of economic growth. On that Committee, Dr Shimomura represented the Ministry of Finance, while his opposite number was Mr Shigeo Matsumoto, representing the Bank of Japan.

The record of that meeting shows that Mr Matsumoto "emphasised the necessity of maintaining the independence or neutrality of the central bank from the government on the ground that the central bank is first of all assigned with the task of contributing to the stabilisation of the currency value….".[22] Meanwhile, Dr Shimomura is reported as having "stressed the inevitable subordination of the central bank to the government from two standpoints – that the policy of the central bank should be managed and operated in full coordination with the general economic policy of the government and that the government on its part is called upon to hold itself responsible to the nation for the outcome of its financial policy." As Kurihara made clear, Shimomura's view prevailed and Japan prospered.

To sum up, the Bank of England should be brought once again under government control. It is unwise for any government to allow any natural monopoly to be fully independent, and the control of credit creation should be such a central aspect of government policy that direct control is required. The operating objectives of the Bank of England, as a central departmental agency of government policy, should be redefined as the promotion of economic growth and full employment, and the control of inflation, within the guidelines of a national industrial plan.

5: COMPETITIVENESS

The 41 economists who wrote to the *Observer* in support of 'Corbynomics' were in little doubt that a 'people's quantitative easing' provided a positive and credible alternative to austerity. However, most recognised that the major obstacle to any policy for expansion (however defined) was that increased consumption (and therefore imports) would intensify the balance of payments constraint – the inevitable consequence of the damaging loss of competitiveness suffered by British industry over many decades.

The impact of that loss of competitiveness on Britain's economic performance and standing has been dramatic. Whereas the British share of world trade in 1950 was a commendable 10.7 per cent, by 2013 it had dropped to just 2.6 per cent. The figures for manufacturers are even more stark. Manufacturing as a contributor to our GDP had been declining steadily but was still nearly a quarter in 1980. Today, reflecting the rapid decline during the years of North Sea oil and the supposed Thatcherite 'reforms', it has fallen much further to just 10 per cent. While consumption is reasonably buoyant, manufacturing continues to contract and is – as we begin 2016 – technically in recession after a third quarter of contraction.

This matters greatly. While much attention is paid to services, 60 per cent of our exports and 80 per cent of our imports are accounted for by goods rather than services. So the smaller proportion of our GDP accounted for by manufacturing is both evidence of, and a major contributor to, our economic decline.

Yet growing our manufacturing is not only the most important source of incremental innovation in a modern economy, the most substantial creator of new jobs, the most effective stimulus to improved productivity and the means of obtaining the quickest return on investment; it also provides great social benefits. To a much greater degree than in the case of, say, financial services, it spreads employment and therefore prosperity both geographically (well beyond, in the case of the UK, the affluent south east) and socially (by providing well-paid jobs to blue-collar workers).

We currently run a deficit, which shows no sign of reducing, of £100bn in our trade in manufactured goods – around 6 per cent of GDP. It is a deficit that arises because we are simply unable to pay our way in the world; and that, in turn, is because it costs more to manufacture in the UK than in most other countries. The 70 per cent of the costs of manufacturing – comprising wages, salaries and profits – that are locally incurred are charged out to the rest of the world at such a high rate that it prices our goods out of world markets. These markets are now dominated by more efficient (such as American, German, Japanese, and Korean), and cheaper (such as China and India) competitors.

There is, however, no intrinsic reason why our goods should be more expensive than others, other than our insistence that they should be. The level at which we charge our costs to customers in the internationally traded goods sector is, in other words, determined by ourselves through the exchange rate we set – it is our decision to price our goods out of world markets, including our own.

Over most of this period, the consequence is that the British economy has been handicapped by a persistent and growing trade deficit. Our last trade surplus was in 1982 and our last current account surplus was in 1983. The perennial trade deficit is a major element in making inevitable the deficit in government finances over which so much effort, concern and ink is spilt, yet the two are virtually never seen as being linked. While the government deficit is the focus of attention, the trade deficit is treated as an apparently natural and quite separate fact of life.

Yet the trade deficit is one of the most important factors not only demonstrating our lack of competitiveness but inhibiting any possibility of policies for sustainable growth, because of the fear that growth would exacerbate both inflation and the need to borrow. The result is that we dare not grow – even in a recession – for fear of balance of trade constraints. We are reduced, for as long as we can find willing lenders and buyers, to financing our unsustainable consumption by overseas borrowing and selling off our assets. That in turn produces a perennial trade gap which has to be financed in the same way.

The problem is easily identified as a loss of international competitiveness, but the solution apparently remains elusive. Even those who understand that British industry needs to invest much more so as to increase output and improve productivity are at a loss as to how to bring it about. Exhortation, tax incentives, direct government action have all been advocated, but none has shown any sign of being effective. Even the most committed supporters of expansion seem to have hit a brick wall.

The exchange rate

Yet the solution is staring us in the face. Just as competitiveness is the single most important determinant of productivity and profitability, and ultimately of living standards, so the exchange rate is the single most important determinant of international competitiveness. This is because the exchange rate converts all domestic costs into prices in the internationally traded goods sector. There is no other factor that has such a direct, inevitable and comprehensive impact on the ability to compete in international markets.

There are those who argue that, in today's global economy, price competitiveness matters little and the competitive edge that makes the difference lies in product quality and meeting the customers' needs. What this argument overlooks is that a lack of ability to compete on price will eventually and inevitably lead in the longer term to comparatively poorer quality and a reduced ability to satisfy the customer. It is, in other words, difficult and eventually impossible to match the foreign competition in quality terms if a lack of price competitiveness, particularly if sustained over a period, means that the profits that are needed to re-invest in improving quality are simply not available. The domestic producer and potential exporter then have the difficult task of trying to sell into international markets goods that are not only more expensive but are increasingly inferior in quality as well.

If the currency is over-valued, those selling against international competition both at home and overseas either have to raise prices and risk losing market share, or have to hold prices and accept reduced margins. Reduced profits (either because of lower sales or narrower margins – or both), if sustained over any length of time, mean less money for re-investment, less growth, less employment, less research on product development, less new technology and equipment, less market research and market development (especially overseas) and less to spend on employing skilled staff, skill training of existing staff, marketing and after-sales service – all the factors that govern success in the internationally traded goods sector, where the real prospects for growth lie.

Perhaps the most obvious, direct and persistent evidence of an over-valued exchange rate, however, is a persistent imbalance in the current account. The trade deficit has to be financed in some way or another. The usual consequence is that both individuals (persons and corporations) and governments have to borrow or sell assets to cover that proportion of the cost of imports that is not covered by exports. In each of these cases, therefore, both governments and countries take on increased debt and this will in turn see the balance of trade problem worsen, as increased interest payments to lenders and repatriated profits to new overseas owners have to cross the foreign exchanges.

In the case of the UK, the sale of overseas assets has reached very large proportions, gathering pace since the global financial crisis and amounting to no less than £615bn in the decade from 2000 to 2010. This inflow of foreign capital, without any matching increase in output, then exacerbates the problem further, since the increased demand for sterling helps to drive up the exchange rate and compound the loss of competitiveness still further.

Excuses for over-valuation

There are always those who, having seen successive devaluations over a long period – devaluations that are virtually always the long-delayed minimum responses to a pre-existing loss of competitiveness that can no longer be sustained – are inclined to think that nothing further is to be done in that direction and do not therefore bother to look at the evidence. We can no doubt expect a similar response to the recent fall in sterling's value, reflecting global uncertainties, from £1 = $1.60 a year ago to £1 = $1.40 today. And the exchange rate's significance is often dismissed because it is asserted that any advantage to competitiveness from a devaluation would be quickly eroded by inflation, and that it would in any case bring about an unacceptable fall in the living standards which would be politically unsustainable.

None of these propositions is true; they are lazily asserted in defiance of the available evidence. My co-author on occasion, John Mills, has shown conclusively in a recent book[23] that devaluation neither causes living standards to fall (but the reverse) nor is it followed by higher inflation. Mills establishes these points by looking first at the economic arguments and then at the empirical evidence.

He has analysed 10 significant devaluations over a decades-long period, ranging from the 24 per cent British devaluation in 1931, through the 28 per cent US devaluation from 1985 to 1987, to the 18 per cent British devaluation of 2007–9. He is able to show that in almost every case, real GDP per head increased significantly in the period following the devaluation. Even in those few cases where GDP fell for a time, it was due to factors such as the global financial crisis rather than the devaluation.

Furthermore, in the aftermath of devaluations, and contrary to almost all predictions (and rarely questioned conventional wisdom), inflation did not soar. This was particularly striking in the case of the British devaluations of 1931 and 1992 when, despite dire warnings, inflation was unaffected. This was also true of the devaluation – since substantially reversed – following 2008.

The record shows that on those occasions when devaluation has become unavoidable, the benefits have confounded the conventional wisdom that they would be quickly lost. In the 1930s, following the abandonment of the Gold Standard and the consequent devaluation of sterling by 28 per cent against the dollar in 1931, the UK economy grew faster than it had ever done or has done since – cumulatively by 3.8 per cent per annum between 1932 and 1937.

Manufacturing output rose over the period by 48 per cent and 2.6 million new jobs were created. But for this, the UK would not have had the strength to fight and win the second world war.

A recent instance of a significant devaluation occurred when the UK was forced by looming economic crisis to leave the Exchange Rate Mechanism in 1992. The outcome of what was in effect a 19 per cent devaluation was that inflation did not rise, as had been predicted, but actually fell. The GDP deflator, a common measure of inflation, was 6.7 per cent in 1991, 4 per cent in 1992, 2.8 per cent in 1993 and just 1.5 per cent a year later. At the same time, real wages rose, after rises of just 0.2 per cent in 1990 and 1.9 per cent in 1991, by a remarkable 7.6 per cent in 1992, before falling back to 1.6 per cent in 1993 and 1.2 per cent in 1994. These were the impressive outcomes of what was actually a typically ex post facto and forced devaluation which achieved only a fraction of what was really needed.

The new economic giants of Asia have not been in any doubt about the advantages of a competitive exchange rate. They have focused on holding down their exchange rates so as to maintain the competitive advantage that rapid industrialisation is able to produce. China, in particular, clearly recognised the importance of holding down the value of the yuan over the whole period of its rapid growth, while Japan, intent on kick-starting a sluggish economy, has taken decisive action in the last few years to bring down the value of the yen by over 30 per cent.

We, however, have constantly sought ways to prop up the pound – and always with the same disastrous results. Nearly a century ago it was the Gold Standard; more recently, attempts have been made to fix parities in the European context. The European 'currency snake', established in 1972, was replaced in 1979 by the European Monetary System which eventually became the Exchange Rate Mechanism (the ERM). These arrangements were designed to allow national governments to argue that decisions on the exchange rate were not their responsibility but were exclusively the prerogative of an unaccountable European central bank; the ERM was eventually abandoned when the damage it did became too evident to be ignored.

This did not deter the ideologues from trying again, however, with the euro. What was proposed this time was that the whole concept of national currencies, each serving the interests of its own national economy, would be terminated. The outcome, predictably enough, was the stagnation of large parts of the eurozone, as they laboured under the burden of an over-valued currency.

A further obstacle to clear analysis is the insistence that the exchange rate should serve as a counter-inflationary tool and that little attention should be paid to its importance as a market-clearing price. As a result, we require the exchange rate to perform two quite different and often contradictory functions, and it is always the more important function – the balancing of our trade – that is sacrificed.

The true function of a correctly aligned exchange rate is to allow the economy to grow at a satisfactory rate, while at the same time ensuring that we are able to make full use of our resources and that – in fulfilment of its fundamental role as a market-clearing price – our trade remains in balance so that growth and innovation are not restrained by balance of payments difficulties.

A further factor is also at work. A devaluation would have the powerful effect of reducing the value of assets, and particularly financial assets. Everyone, in other words, and not just wage-earners, would be required to make their contribution to the improvement in competitiveness. This is a sacrifice too far for the holders of assets and the drawers of profits who prefer to focus on driving down wages, which – while ineffective to improve competitiveness by much – at least has the merit from their viewpoint of preserving and often reinforcing their differential privilege.

A theoretical issue also arises. Classical economists believed that issues of demand and competitiveness were irrelevant and that, if unemployment occurred, it was because the labour market was functioning badly, in the sense that workers were demanding wages that were too high. Keynesian economics, however, offers a different perspective.

Keynes' argument was that unemployment arose because there was a lack of what he called effective demand in the economy. He defined effective demand as a matter of expectation – the perceived future willingness and ability of people to buy the goods that were to be produced at a price that would be more profitable, in light of the foreseen costs of production, than would be the rate of interest.

If effective demand were deficient, government intervention by increasing the purchasing power of prospective purchasers in the market place would be needed so as to increase the likelihood that they would buy the products that the producer was about to make. With demand at an adequate level, Keynes argued, the supply of goods would rise to meet the demand; and if that were the case, this would invalidate and indeed reverse Say's Law – one of the cardinal principles of classical economics – which held that supply would inevitably and always create its own equivalent demand.

What is surprising, however, is that Keynes' account of how effective demand might operate took little account of competitiveness. By the 1930s, after all, it was clear that the increasing role played and inroads made by powerful manufacturing rivals – including the United States, Germany and Japan – was bound to have a depressing effect on the level of demand for domestically produced British goods in both home and overseas markets. Keynes' hypothetical prospective investor (and employer), in considering what demand there would be for his product, was surely bound to take account of the competition from highly efficient rivals which would directly affect the price he would be able to charge.

If they were able to take part of his domestic market from him, or keep him out of markets overseas, or force him to reduce his prices and margins in any part of the internationally traded goods market, either at home or abroad, this would surely be a major factor in the kind of expectations he might have about the wisdom of investing. And as the volume of world trade has grown, and import penetration has increased substantially, the lack of competitiveness of the British productive sector has inevitably been a major factor in determining the level of effective demand in the domestic economy, and makes the application of Keynesian prescriptions in order to achieve full employment virtually impossible.

It is this largely overlooked factor which explains much of our economic history over recent decades. Jim Callaghan's famous statement to the Labour Conference in 1976 that "you can't spend your way out of a recession" seemed to be an overt admission by the prime minister that, in his view and in the view of his advisers, Keynesianism was then a busted flush. The combination of slow growth and threatened and increasing inflation known as 'stagflation' seemed impervious to Keynesian remedies.

The obvious remedy for rising unemployment and sluggish output and productivity was, in accordance with Keynes' theories about effective demand, to use the power of government to intervene by means of increased spending. But that remedy was precluded because any increase in spending would stimulate inflation even further than the point to which the oil-price shock and Heath's unwise index-ation of wages had brought it. It would also, as increased spending power sucked in more imports, worsen a growing balance of trade problem.

Little wonder, then, that Jim Callaghan declared that he and his government had run into a cul de sac, and that Denis Healey was forced to make a humiliating emergency car ride back from the airport to address the Labour conference, followed by an equally humiliating application to the IMF for help. The rest of the world watched – astonished – as Keynes was in effect, repudiated in his own homeland, and by a government of the left.

Healey preferred instead to adopt monetarist orthodoxy and the defence of sterling as the key features of his Chancellorship. The consequences of this policy were disastrous and led, via the "winter of discontent", directly to the election victory of Margaret Thatcher. This ushered in the suite of monetarist and free-market policies that decimated British manufacturing, meant even greater reliance on the shifting sands of the City of London, and – in due course – produced the excesses that created the global financial crisis and the great recession. It lives on, of course, in the policies of austerity that are thought to be appropriate to deal with recession.

Yet it need not have been like this. If the Keynesian econom-ics applied in post-war Britain had taken account of competi-tiveness as a factor in determining effective demand, the brick wall apparently confronting Jim Callaghan and Denis Healey would have been seen to have had no substance. Keynesian analysis retained all of its force as a guide to what was needed to produce and sustain full employment; but it would not work if an essential element in determining the level of effective demand was overlooked and omitted from the policy prescription. We are in danger of continuing these errors to this day.

What needs to be done and would it work?

Healey's dilemma apparently faces the advocates of expansion today. A lack of competitiveness and the consequent balance of payments constraint seem to preclude any lift in economic activity, such as might be brought about by the investment credit creation strategy advocated here. Yet the solution is clear. We should directly address our lack of competitiveness by the most obvious and effective means available – that is, by bringing about a substantial devaluation of the currency. If we accept this conclusion, what should an appropriate level of devaluation be, if we are to secure the benefits we need? And what assurance do we have that they would be secured?

The widely accepted condition for the effectiveness of a devaluation is known as the Marshall-Lerner condition, and requires that the sum of the price elasticities for imports and exports is greater than unity. That condition is easily met in our case and shows that our economic performance can be significantly improved and the current account constraint removed by a fall in the pound's value from its current level of about £1.00 = $1.40 to £1.00 = $1.10, with the same reduction applying against all currencies. That is, a devaluation of about 21 per cent, which is lower than the 28 per cent fall in 1931 against the US dollar, when the UK came off the Gold Standard.

Both that precedent from our own experience and the recent fall in the Japanese yen show clearly that bringing the exchange rate down on this scale can be done by a determined government.

A devaluation of this size[24] would re-balance the UK economy towards manufacturing, investment and exports to the extent required to provide improvements in both the overall growth rate and the current account balance. A devaluation on a lesser scale, or one that was quickly reversed, would have much less effect, even proportionately, since it would do much less to change expectations and thence behaviour.

Importantly, this level of devaluation would also be needed to allow household expenditure to increase modestly at the same time so that consequential improvements in living standards throughout the transitional period could be achieved. This is a vital requirement if the proposed change in economic strategy is to be generally acceptable to the electorate. Voters should be assured that the strategy to secure a better economic performance would not require the sacrifice of living standards, even in the short term.

The foreign payments deficit would be eliminated in three years – or a little longer if we were prepared to sustain consumer spending by further borrowing over a short period. There would be a short-term increase in the deficit, which would no doubt help to get the external value of sterling down, before the current account stabilised with a relatively small surplus.

Inflation, as measured by the consumer price index (CPI), could be expected to rise a little from its current level and then to stabilise at 3 per cent per annum. While, as we have seen, it is widely believed that devaluations always produce increased inflation, and import prices would have to rise, strong disinflationary factors would also kick in to help hold inflation down.

A lower exchange rate would, for example, allow both market interest rates and taxation to be reduced from their pre-existing levels. Production runs would increase, allowing economies of scale, and productivity increases in manufacturing would rise sharply as increased investment came on stream. Sourcing would become more locally focused, moving away from more expensive foreign suppliers. These counter-inflationary factors are no more than the expected market responses to an increased competitiveness of domestic production, whether achieved by devaluation or otherwise.

The boost to export volumes and to import substitution would substantially increase the size of available markets, both at home and abroad, and therefore lift the level of effective demand. The improvement in profitability and the stimulus to investment and manufacturing capacity in particular would lift employment and wages and further strengthen demand and, as Keynes asserted, supply would grow to meet that greater demand – a demand that would be met, in view of improved competitiveness, from the domestic economy rather than from overseas.

The projected increase in consumer expenditure does not allow for any increase in the population. If the UK population continues to rise at around 0.6 per cent per annum, as it has done on average for the last four years, then the increase in GDP per head per year would be closer to 3 per cent a year. Productivity increases may take a little time to pick up to a higher rate than their historical average of about 2 per cent per annum, so that there would be an immediate and cumulative increase in the demand for labour. Registered unemployment would fall by about 400,000 a year or more for two or three years, reducing its level towards 3 per cent, although the total employed labour force would rise by about 50 per cent more than this, by an aggregate of 600,000 per year. Increasing the size of the labour force, buttressed by much higher levels of investment, would be a crucial element in the strategy to get the economy to transition to a much higher growth rate.

Increasing export volumes and import substitution, would lift the proportion of GDP delivered by manufacturing from 10.7 per cent in 2012 to about 13 per cent in 2018. Gross investment would need to rise from the inadequate 14 per cent of GDP, where it is at the moment, to well over 20 per cent, and the increase could not be spent at the same time on consumption. An increase in output, and a programme of investment credit creation, would make it possible for this to happen, while still allowing household expenditure to increase by the average of 3 per cent per annum.

The increased growth rate would exceed the growth in the country's and the government's debts, with the result that they would stabilise at a level that was sustainable over the longer term. Government revenues and expenditure could be expected to stabilise at a manageable 40 per cent of the increased GDP.

These outcomes, calculated from a carefully worked exemplification of what a 25 per cent devaluation would achieve, would be hugely more acceptable than anything that could be reasonably predicted if we continue on our present course. Without an expansionist strategy, (whether achieved with – as seems essential – or without a substantial devaluation), growth in the economy is unlikely even to keep up with population growth, leading to stagnant or even declining living standards as far ahead as can be envisaged.

CONCLUSION: BRINGING THE ELEMENTS TOGETHER

This pamphlet has looked at two of the major deficiencies in western, and particularly British, economic policy-making: the blind spot on competitiveness, and the dismissal of the real possibilities and true role of monetary policy and credit creation. The question then arises: are these two issues completely independent of each other, so that they need to be addressed separately? Or are they linked in some way so that they can be brought together into a coherent whole, and if so, how?

The answer is that the two are linked, and that they not only reinforce each other but that the one is the necessary corollary of the other, if they are to form the basis of a successful (and alternative) economic policy. They are, in other words, two sides of the same coin.

Just as a tighter monetary policy will cause the exchange rate to rise, the corollary – that a looser monetary policy would cause the exchange rate to fall – is also likely to be true. A contractionary monetary policy – whether achieved directly by raising interest rates or by the central bank selling securities or restricting bank lending – will have the effect of causing interest rates to rise and the price of securities to fall. The result will be an increased demand for those securities (and the higher interest rates) from abroad and therefore an increased inflow of foreign capital. That increase will in turn push up the value of the domestic currency in response to the increased demand.

The reverse is true for an expansionary monetary policy. Lower interest rates and a higher price for securities will mean a reduced demand from abroad for those securities, a correspondingly lower inflow of foreign currency and lower demand for the domestic currency, and therefore a lower value for that currency.

Moreover, a tight monetary policy will not only be associated with the reality of higher interest rates. It will also suggest a supposedly low-risk and business-friendly policy stance, an adherence to neo-classical doctrine, and a monetary approach that means in principle little or no growth in the money supply. The 'confidence' thereby engendered (usually reinforced by declarations from the government of its determination to protect the currency, by the capital movements that flow from the priority given to the City's role as a financial centre, and the favourable tax treatment of UK land and other assets) will encourage the purveyors of 'hot money' to entrust their short-term capital to what seems to be a safe and high-yield location.

The reverse will also be true. The prospect of new money being created, low interest rates, and a proclaimed determination to lower the value of the currency (as has been the case in Japan) would see the holders of sterling running for cover. The Japanese experience shows how effective this can be in achieving a depreciation. There is, after all, no such thing as a clean float; the markets will always react to the various stimuli placed before them.

The money markets will initially react adversely to monetary expansion with its apparently inflationary risks. But they will over time – as they see that expansion does not go to asset inflation in the housing market, but to increased and more competitive production – regain their appetite for securities offered by the domestic economy. Any rise in the exchange rate at that point, however, would be on the basis of a stronger economy and a better understanding of the growth path on which the economy is then set.

The combined strategy of providing increased funding for productive investment and encouraging that investment through improving competitiveness provides a coherent strategy. It would offer a real choice to the voters and enthuse those who are keen for change, without departing in any way from mainstream economics. The overall strategy is recognisably Keynesian and would be supported by that growing group of economists that is now confident that neo-liberalism as an economic doctrine has had its day.

Most importantly, it means that those who increasingly understand the failures of neo-liberalism are not discouraged by a reluctance to tackle the doctrine on the centrally important territory where its deficiencies are most apparent and damaging. The left's inability to offer an alternative economic strategy – whether the consequence of a failure of analysis or of courage – would no longer hand over the economic argument – uncontested – to the beneficiaries of the current orthodoxy. A credible alternative will never win the argument, however, if its proponents are too frightened to advance it. An economic strategy built on these elements would not only produce a better economic performance but would – properly explained and understood – commend itself to the electorate as well, provided that they get a chance to see it.

Endnotes

1. Money Creation in the Modern Economy, by Michael McLeay, Amar Radla and Ryland Thomas.

2. Galbraith, J. K. (1976) *Money: Whence it Came, Where it Went*, Harmondsworth, Penguin.

3. Phillips, R. (1995) *The Chicago Plan & New Deal Banking Reform*, London, M.E. Sharpe.

4. Kotlikoff, L. (2010) *Jimmy Stewart Is Dead: Ending the World's Ongoing Financial Plague with Limited Purpose Banking*, Hoboken, John Wiley & Sons.

5. Ryan-Collins, J., Greenham, T., Werner, R. and Jackson, A. (2011) *Where Does Money Come From? A Guide to the UK Monetary and Banking System*, London, New Economics Foundation. Jackson, A. and Dyson, B. (2012) *Modernising Money: Why Our Monetary System is Broken and How it Can Be Fixed*, London, Positive Money.

6. Wolf, M. (2014) 'Strip private banks of their power to create money', *Financial Times* 24.4.2014.

7. Phillips, R. (1995) *The Chicago Plan & New Deal Banking Reform*, London, M.E. Sharpe.

8. www.renewal.org.uk/articles/modern-money-and-the-escape-from-austerity

9. Wray, L. (2014) 'What are taxes for? The MMT approach', *New Economic Perspectives* 15.5.2014, at http://neweconomicperspectives.org/2014/05/taxes-mmt-approach.html.

10. Pettifor, A. (2014) *Just Money: How Society Can Break the Despotic Power of Finance*, London, Commonwealth.

11. See Minsky, H. (2013) *Ending Poverty: Jobs, Not Welfare*, Annandale-on-Hudson, Levy Economics Institute.

12. Brown, E. (2012) *The Web of Debt: The Shocking Truth About Our Money System and How We Can Break Free*, Baton Rouge, Third Millennium. Brown, E. (2013) *The Public Bank Solution: From Austerity to Prosperity*, Baton Rouge, Third Millennium.

13. See www.voxeu.org/article/helicopter-money-policy-option

14. I am indebted to my colleague, George Tait Edwards, who drew my attention to Shimomura's importance and has worked for years to interest Western economists in Shimomura's work.

15. "The Growth Potential of the Japanese Economy" (John Hopkins Press Maryland 1971), p.61

16. New Paradigm in Macroeconomics, Richard A. Werner. Palgrave Macmillan, 2005

17. See: Adair Turner, Between Debt and the Devil, Princeton University Press, 2015

18. www.oecd.org/eco/outlook/focusonhouseprices.htm

19. www.bankofengland.co.uk/financialstability/Pages/fpc/loanincome.aspx

20. www.levyinstitute.org/pubs/wp_805.pdf, O. Giovannoni, What Do We Know About The Labor Share and The Profit Share?; and more generally, Joseph Stiglitz, The Price of Inequality, Norton, 2012

21. James Forder, 'Why Is Central Bank Independence So Widely Approved', *Journal of Economic Issues*, December 2005

22. From "The Political Economy of Japanese Monetary Policy" by Thomas E Cargill, Michael M Hutchinson and Takatoshi Ito, The MIT Press, Cambridge Massachusetts and London, England, p24.

23. John Mills, Exchange Rate Alignments, Palgrave Macmillan, 2012. See too: John Mills and Bryan Gould, Call To Action, W.H.Allen, 2015

24. The basis for all of the calculations in this section is a carefully worked exemplification by my co-author, John Mills, of what a 30% devaluation from the then sterling/US dollar rate of £1.00 = $1.60 to £1.00 = $1.10 could achieve. Some part of that devaluation has already been achieved. See John Mills and Bryan Gould, Call To Action, W.H.Allen, 2015

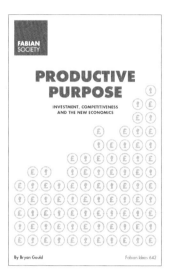

Productive Purpose
Investment, competitiveness and the new economics

How to use this Discussion Guide

The guide can be used in various ways by Fabian Local Societies, local political party meetings and trade union branches, student societies, NGOs and other groups.

- You might hold a discussion among local members or invite a guest speaker – for example, an MP, academic or local practitioner to lead a group discussion.

- Some different key themes are suggested. You might choose to spend 15–20 minutes on each area, or decide to focus the whole discussion on one of the issues for a more detailed discussion.

A discussion could address some or all of the following questions:

1. Is quantitative easing a non-inflationary and viable economic policy to boost investment? If so, how can Labour avoid the charge of printing money and fiscal irresponsibility?

2. The pamphlet argues that a national industrial strategy is seen as a prime requirement in other more successful economies. What would one look like for the UK and how could it avoid the charge of 'picking winners'?

3. Should Labour make the case for devaluing our currency to boost competitiveness in global markets?

Please let us know what you think

Whatever view you take of the issues, we would very much like to hear about your discussion. Please send us a summary of your debate (perhaps 300 words) to debate@fabians.org.uk.

JOIN BRITAIN'S ONLY MEMBERSHIP THINK TANK

Members of the Fabian Society receive at least four pamphlets or books a year as well as our quarterly magazine, 'Fabian Review'. You'll also receive invitations to special members' events and regular lectures and debates with leading politicians and thinkers.

For just £3.50 a month you can join now and we'll send you two pamphlets and the latest magazine free.

Call 020 7227 4900, email us at info@fabians.org.uk, or go to www.fabians.org.uk for more information.